Olga **Korbut**
Ольга **Корбут**

GYMNASTICS TRAILBLAZER

Olga**Korbut**
Ольга**Корбут**

GYMNASTICS TRAILBLAZER

BY Christine**Dzidrums**

GymnStars Volume 10

Creative Media Publishing

CREATIVE MEDIA, INC.
PO Box 6270
Whittier, California 90609-6270
United States of America

Book & cover design by Joseph Dzidrums

www.creativemedia.net

First Edition: August 2016

LCCN: On File
ISBN 978-1-938438-95-0
eISBN: 978-1-933438-96-7

To Ashley,
My Little Gymnast

TABLE OF CONTENTS

"When you touch the equipment ... that's it - you're in."

1955 introduced several groundbreaking legends that shaped the world. In the momentous year, Dodgers Sandy Koufax ascended his first Major League Baseball pitching mound. Disneyland opened their gates in Anaheim, California. An exhilarating singer named Elvis Presley riveted audiences during his first television appearance.

Meanwhile, Olympic champion Olga Korbut was born in 1955. The Belarusian pixie would electrify the world at the Munich Olympics with her endearing personality and revolutionary gymnastics moves. She would eventually become known as the *Mother of Modern Gymnastics*.

"Spectators have always been my best judges."

Olga Valentinovna Korbut entered the world on May 16, 1955, in Grodno, Belarus. The youngest child had a trio of sisters: Ludmilla, Zemfira, and Irina. Her father, Valentin, a World War II veteran met her mother, Valentina, while he was recovering at a hospital where she volunteered.

Olga means "blessed, holy; successful." However, the Korbuts affectionately called their youngest member: Dochka. The endearing term means "little girl" in Russian.

The Korbuts did not lead a privileged life. The poor family crammed into a one-bedroom, 180-square foot home.

Mother and father logged many hours at their jobs. An engineer, Valentin rarely complained about his monetary troubles. Meanwhile, Valentina earned money as a cook in a canteen.

Valentin

Valentina

Irina

Zemfira

Ludmilla

Olga

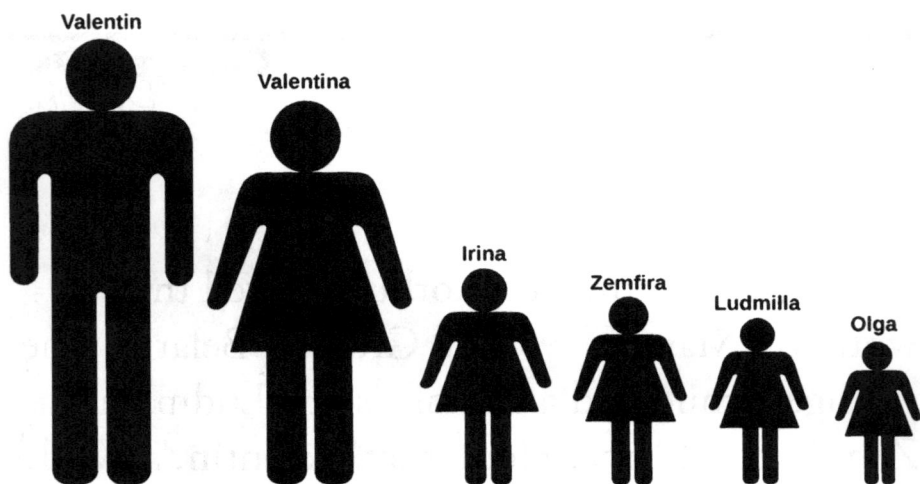

Because they had two working parents, the Korbut children were self-sufficient at a young age. They cared for themselves for long hours. Usually around eleven o'clock at night, an exhausted mother and father returned home to tuck the children into their beds.

Despite growing up with little money, Olga never desired much. The cheerful, upbeat girl spent many fond afternoons playing outdoors with her sisters and neighborhood children. She particularly loved garnering attention from her playmates.

"Watch me do a cartwheel," she ordered the other kids.

A fierce competitor, Olga possessed an unquenchable desire to excel at everything. She ran faster than her peers, spoke louder than them, and laughed stridently. When children scaled trees on scorching summer days, the tomboy always out climbed them all.

On one occasion, Olga watched a little boy stuff seven plums into his mouth. Brimming with showmanship, the enthusiastic youngster saw an opportunity to outshine her friend. She plucked a handful of plums from a nearby tree and waved them at her wide-eyed pals.

"I can fit eight plums into my mouth," she triumphantly announced.

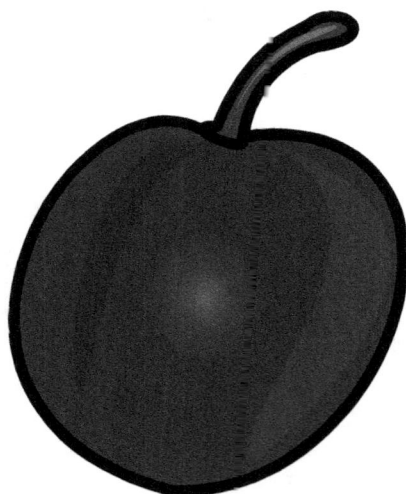

Olga made good on her promise, but she nearly regretted the decision when the plums became jammed in her slight mouth. Her terrified green eyes bulged as she choked on the food. Her tiny fingers couldn't remove the fruit from her mouth fast enough.

Then, a lightbulb went off in the girl's head. Suddenly, she formed two fists with her hands and squished her cheeks with them. Plum bits flew everywhere, but Olga could breathe again. Most importantly, she had won the showdown.

Thankfully, Olga eventually found an ideal outlet for her stubborn, competitive nature, and gymnastics would soon welcome its first superstar.

*"I was smiling from my heart.
I was crying from my heart."*

On a chilly October morning, Olga wiggled and twitched at her desk in her second-grade classroom. The youngster felt too restless to focus on her Russian language lesson. As if fate declared it, a door opened and changed her life.

Yaroslav Korol, the physical education teacher, spoke to the intrigued classroom. The school had created its first gymnastics program. It would offer lessons twice a week.

"Who wants to sign up for classes?" Mr. Korol asked.

A wide grin spread across Olga's animated face. She raised her tiny hand and waved it excitedly. The little girl left little doubt that she wanted to join the class.

Olga thought gymnastics resembled the circus. She had always dreamed of tumbling like an acrobat and showing the balance skills of a tightrope walker! With gymnastics, the youngster

Little Olga

could learn acrobatics on the floor exercise and master precision on the balance beam.

The Korbuts had gone to the circus years earlier. Afterward, Olga spent many hours pretending she was performing in a show under the big top. The youngster dreamed of becoming a circus artist.

One afternoon, Olga's mother sent her to the store to buy milk. On the walk home, the little girl placed the container on top of her head and spun in place as fast as possible. It stayed in place! Buoyed by success, she repeated the trick, but the pitcher fell, spilling milk all over her.

On the first day of class, Olga tried not to fidget as Mr. Korol lectured on the history of gymnastics. Why wouldn't he stop talking and teach them tricks? She couldn't wait to dance across the foam mats and fly through the air in a tumbling series. If the teacher would stop speaking, Olga could learn the moves she admired!

Finally, the teacher's speech ended, and he asked his new students to rise. Olga jumped to her feet. She licked her lips excitedly and eyed the equipment with glee.

Olga was a standout gymnast. She owned natural talent and worked harder, too. The athlete absorbed elementary moves quickly, mastering them with a maturity that belied her tender years.

Olga felt overjoyed when her instructor challenged her with extra exercises. She nailed those, too. The gifted athlete even modeled various elements to show others how to do them properly.

"I need more time to learn skills," Olga thought. "Why can't I train more than twice a week?"

Eventually, Mr. Korol entered his class in the Grodno City Gymnastics Meet. Unable to afford the standard uniform, Olga transformed a t-shirt into a leotard using a safety pin. In the end, Olga's team placed in the top three.

After the competition had concluded, coaches from various sports schools asked the girls to stand in a straight line. One by one, the instructors picked girls that they wanted to train full-time in gymnastics.

Olga did not expect anyone to select her. Then, Elena Volchetskaya, a 1964 Olympic gold medalist with the Soviet team, approached the youngest Korbut

"Want to go to a sports school?" she asked.

The tiny girl's heart soared with happiness. Did she want to attend a gymnastics school full time and take lessons from an Olympic champion?

It was only her biggest dream!

Flag of the Union of Soviet Socialist Republics

*"I brought a new
gymnastics to the world."*

Olga couldn't stop smiling during her first year at gymnastics school. She finally had time to train to her heart's content. The young gymnast embraced practices, showing a great hunger to learn difficult skills and improve her technique.

Elena Volchetskaya believed deeply in her beginner student even when others did not. Head coach Renald Ivanovich Knysh, Ren for short, claimed Olga would never be a champion because she wasn't lean enough.

"I don't understand why you keep her," he told the other instructor.

"Olga works hard and learns quickly," Elena argued. "She will stay."

A month later, Ren watched Olga carefully. She had improved so much in just four weeks. The coach knew the gymnast worked hard, too, so he invited her to join his elite group.

Olga felt thrilled to work under Ren's guidance. The experienced instructor coached students that competed in international meets. He could help her reach world and Olympic events.

Student and coach often argued at first. Olga was an outgoing adolescent who wore her emotions on her sleeve. On the other hand, Ren was quiet and reserved. No one ever knew the thoughts behind his calm expressions.

Working with Ren felt like riding a wild roller coaster. The coach mostly ignored Olga. Sometimes, he watched her but acted unimpressed by even her hardest skills.

On one occasion, several gymnasts were trying to learn a backward somersault on the balance beam. Few girls in the world could accomplish the tricky move. When Olga jumped onto the apparatus and performed the skill cleanly, her training partners squealed with delight.

"Ren," they called. "Olga did a somersault on the balance beam. Did you see it?"

"So what?" the instructor replied. "Warm up."

Years later, Olga realized that Ren faked disinterest to see if she would give up or keep working. The gymnast always responded to his indifference by training harder to gain his attention. Her efforts finally convinced him that she had serious talent and determination.

Olga was a strong girl who never backed down from challenges. A grumpy instructor would not derail her dreams, nor would the biggest injury of her gymnastics career.

Olga fell one day on the balance beam and dislocated her arm. When the doctor removed her cast following surgery, she could barely move her limb. He had forgotten to give her exercises to do, and it became stuck in a bent position. When physical exercise didn't correct the damage, the gymnast made sand bags and slept with them on her arm every night. Finally, her limb straightened, and she resumed training.

Olga felt a surge of confidence after overcoming her significant injury. Nothing would hold her back. She perfected a backflip on the balance beam and invented several new moves.

Olga also developed the Korbut Flip on the uneven bars. In the groundbreaking move, she stood on the high bar, performed a backflip, and grasped the bar again. When the gymnast completed the move at her first major meet, it helped her win the all-around event.

Additionally, Ren encouraged Olga to smile more. If she maintained a straight expression, people would notice the tricks' difficulties. Elements look easier if a gymnast looked happy.

So, Olga always smiled, whether she performed a flawless skill or fell. Cheerful behavior

The Korbut Flip

came easily to her. Before long, audiences began smiling back at the charming girl with the mega-watt grin.

In 1969, Olga competed in the Soviet National Gymnastics Championships against several Olympians. Despite being a newcomer, she gained many new fans at the event. People marveled at her tricky moves and outgoing personality. Enthusiastic audiences cheered wildly during her routines.

The crowd booed when the judges did not award Olga the win. Many wanted explanations for her fifth-place finish in the all-around.

Experts speculated that Olga was paying the price for paving the way for a new style of gymnastics. The sport historically favored older women with balletic looks, and the young girl's powerful, fast, and flashy style confused judges. The gymnast's unique talent made scoring her difficult!

Several months after nationals, Olga attended a national training camp in Leselidze, a town located near the Black Sea. For a week, the teenager trained alongside her idols. Larissa Latynina, a former gymnast with 18 Olympic medals, ran the Soviet women's gymnastics program. The legend was also responsible for selecting the international teams. At the end of camp, she named young Korbut as the first alternate for the 1970 World Championships.

Olga felt devastated at missing the world team. However, she turned her disappointment into resolve, vowing to compete at the Olympics.

When she and Ren returned home, they resumed working hard. They continued creating innovative moves that pushed the boundary of the sport. Their solid work consistently made the gymnast a fan favorite wherever she competed.

Their efforts paid off at the 1972 Soviet Nationals when Olga placed third in the all-around competition. Months later, she won gold at the USSR Cup. Encouraged by her results, the Soviet Union's gymnastics federation named her to the Olympic team.

Olga Korbut had finally arrived on the gymnastics' scene in a big way.

Next stop: the Munich Olympics.

Olga Charms the Audience

"I loved the thrill and pressure of competition and the everyday pursuit of perfection."

Olga arrived at the 1972 Munich Olympics hoping to win several medals. Because Ren wasn't an official team coach, he could not stand on the floor with Olga. Instead, he traveled to Munich as a spectator and spoke to his student in between practices.

Olga's first medal was golden when the Soviet Union won the team competition by nearly four points. East Germany took the silver medal, and Hungary placed third. The Soviet's victory marked their sixth straight Olympic team title.

The German crowd supported every gymnast, but they showered great affection on Olga. The Soviet gymnast became a quick favorite thanks to her spellbinding skills and dazzling personality.

"Ol-ga, Ol-ga, Ol-ga!" the crowd cheered whenever the seventeen-year-old took the floor.

Queen of the Munich Olympics

During the short time between the end of the team and all-around competitions, Olga suffered a back injury. The teenager missed several practices as she laid in bed recuperating. Eventually, doctors gave her an approved painkiller which helped relieve some discomfort.

Unfortunately, the lost training time hurt Olga in the all-around competition. During the first element on her favorite event, the uneven bars, Olga slipped on the matting. A few seconds later, she fumbled a second time, Then, the gymnast made a third error. The surprised crowd oohed in disappointment. Like that, the teen sensation's chance of winning the all-around gold had disintegrated.

"Even with her mistakes, she's still revolutionizing gymnastics," an American commentator raved.

München  1972

Soviet gymnasts were known for their composed and calm behavior under the pressure of competition. If they made errors, their stoic faces showed little reaction; if they excelled, they never looked excited. It seemed that neither good nor bad performances affected them.

Olga stood out from her contemporaries. After her mistakes in the all-around competition, the devastated youngster dissolved into tears. Audiences were moved to see a Soviet gymnast show genuine emotion. Millions rallied behind the "Sparrow from Minsk," as they nicknamed her, and transformed her into an overnight star.

Golden Girl

Although Ludmilla Tourischeva won the all-around, Olga garnered the lion's share of attention. The seventh-place finisher captured newspaper headlines and dominated Olympic talk everywhere. People wanted to see her win an individual event.

Olga had the chance to win another Olympic medal in the uneven bars event. The youngster performed a thrilling routine complete with the Korbut Flip. Her efforts earned her a silver medal.

Olga's two remaining events were the uneven bars and floor exercise. The pixie delivered sparkling performances that dazzled as brightly as her trademark smile. She ultimately scored gold medals in both events, making the audience explode with cheers.

When the 1972 Munich Games ended, the gymnast had scored three gold medals and one silver. More importantly to her, she had won the hearts of the world.

Wax Figure at Madame Tussauds, London
Nevit Dilmen

"Someday, another Olga will be born & perform. I can't wait to witness it."

Olga's fame skyrocketed after the Munich Olympics. Fans constantly mobbed the teenager for autographs whenever she went outside. Eventually, she disguised herself with a black wig and a big hat, but people still recognized her!

The Olympic champion was in high demand following Munich. After starring in a German gymnastics tour, she visited the United States. Big crowds greeted Olga when she landed in airports in different cities, like Los Angeles, Washington D.C., and Chicago. President Richard Nixon also invited the famous athlete for a White House visit.

After Olga returned to the Soviet Union, she and Ren ended their partnership when he suggested that she should retire. Hoping to compete in another Olympics, the teenager started training under a former gymnast named Tamara Stepanova Alexayeva. She appreciated her new coach's quiet, kind demeanor, and the two wom-

Meeting President Richard Nixon

en became good friends.

Olga returned to high-stakes competition at the 1974 World Championships and electrified audiences with stirring routines. The famous gymnast won team and vault gold medals; she also placed second in the all-around, balance beam, uneven bars, and floor exercise.

Olga even unveiled a new vault, the 360-plus-360, at the event. In the daring move, the gymnast performed a 360-degree turn before pushing off the horse and executed another 360-degree turn right before the landing. Her fellow competitors were so impressed that they gave her a standing ovation!

During this time, Olga also furthered her education. She studied history at Grodno State University through independent study. The gymnast completed homework during her free time.

Olga arrived at the 1976 Montreal Olympics with another injury. As a result, she had to remove several difficult skills from her routines.

Despite the setback, Olga helped the Soviet Union win a team gold medal. Romania finished in second place, and East Germany rounded out the podium. The focused gymnast also picked up a silver medal in the balance beam final.

At the White House

Ultimately, Olga won her fourth Olympic gold medal when the Soviet Union captured the team event crown. Rounding out the podium, Romania fin-ished in second place, and East Germany placed third. The focused gymnast also picked up a silver medal in the balance beam final.

Montréal 1976

Following the 1976 Olympics, Olga re-tired from gymnastics. A year later, the sports hero graduated from college. Then, she coached young gymnasts for several years.

In 1978, Olga married Leonid Bortkevich, a member of the Soviet Belarusian folk rock group Pesniary. A year later, the couple welcomed a son, Richard, into their lives. In 1991, the family moved to Georgia in the United States.

The Bortkevich's marriage lasted 23 years before ending in 2000. After the divorce, Olga earned U.S. citizenship and moved to Arizona.

Happily settled in Scottsdale, the four-time Olympic champion offered private lessons at the city's gymnastics facility. Additionally, she delivered motivational speeches on occasion. Her Olympic story always inspired audiences.

Decades after Olga competed in Munich, the Korbut Flip was banned from competition. The reason? It was too dangerous. The decision illustrated just one example of the gymnast's revolutionary role in the sport.

When Olga competed at the Munich Olympics, she hoped to show the world a new form of gymnastics. She did more than that. She changed the direction of the sport forever, and its athletes will always cherish her as the groundbreaker who started it all.

COMPETITIVE RECORD

1969 USSR GYMNASTICS CHAMPIONSHIPS
All-Around - 5

1970 USSR GYMNASTICS CHAMPIONSHIPS
All-Around - 4

1971 USSR GYMNASTICS CHAMPIONSHIPS
All-Around - 4

1972 USSR GYMNASTICS CHAMPIONSHIPS
All-Around - 3

1972 USSR CUP
All-Around - 1

1972 OLYMPICS
Team - 1
Balance Beam - 1
Floor Exercise - 1
Uneven Bars - 2

1973 MOSCOW UNIVERSIAD
All-Around - 1

1973 EUROPEAN CHAMPIONSHIPS
All-Around - 2

1974 WORLD CHAMPIONSHIPS
Team - 1
All-Around - 2
Vault - 1
Uneven Bars -2
Balance Beam - 2
Floor Exercise - 2

1976 OLYMPICS
Team - 1
Balance Beam - 2

Official Website
olgakorbut.com

Official Facebook
facebook.com/olga.korbut.9

Official Twitter Account
twitter.com/olgakorbut1

Official Olympics Website
olympic.org

International Gymnastics Hall of Fame
www.ighof.com

ABOUT THE AUTHOR

Christine Dzidrums has written biographies on many inspiring personalities: *Simone Biles, Clayton Kershaw, Mike Trout, Yuna Kim, Shawn Johnson, Nastia Liukin, The Fierce Five, Gabby Douglas, Sutton Foster, Kelly Clarkson, Idina Menzel* and *Missy Franklin.* Christine's first Young Adult novel, *Cutters Don't Cry*, won a Moonbeam Children's Book Award. Her follow-up to *Cutters, Kaylee: The "What If?" Game*, won a gold medal at the Children's Literary Classic Awards. She also wrote the tween book *Fair Youth* and the beginning reader books *Future Presidents Club* and the *Princess Dessabelle* series. Ms. Dzidrums lives in Southern California with her husband and three children.

www.ChristineDzidrums.com
@ChristineWriter

Now sports fans can learn about gymnastics' greatest stars! Americans **Shawn Johnson** and **Nastia Liukin** became the darlings of the 2008 Beijing Olympics when the fearless gymnasts collected 9 medals between them. Four years later at the 2012 London Olympics, America's **Fab Five** claimed gold in the team competition. A few days later, **Gabby Douglas** added another gold medal to her collection when she became the fourth American woman in history to win the Olympic all-around title. The *GymnStars* series reveals these gymnasts' long, arduous path to Olympic glory. *Gabby Douglas: Golden Smile, Golden Triumph* received a **2012 Moonbeam Children's Book Award**.

At the 2010 Vancouver Olympics, tragic circumstances thrust **Joannie Rochette** into the spotlight when her mother died two days before the ladies short program. Joannie then captured hearts everywhere by courageously skating two moving programs to win the Olympic bronze medal. *Joannie Rochette: Canadian Ice Princess* profiles the popular figure skater's moving journey.

Meet figure skating's biggest star: **Yuna Kim**. The Korean trailblazer produced two legendary performances at the 2010 Vancouver Olympic Games to win the gold medal. *Yuna Kim: Ice Queen* uncovers the compelling story of how the beloved figure skater overcame poor training conditions, various injuries and numerous other obstacles to become world and Olympic champion.

Our ***YNot Girl*** series chronicles the lives and careers of the world's most famous role models. ***Jennie Finch: Softball Superstar*** details the California native's journey from a shy youngster to softball's most famous face. In ***Kelly Clarkson: Behind Her Hazel Eyes***, young readers will find inspiration reading about the superstar's rise from a broke waitress with big dreams to becoming one of the recording industry's top musical acts. ***Missy Franklin: Swimming Sensation*** narrates the Colorado native's transformation from a talented swimming toddler to queen of the pool.

Theater fans first fell for **Sutton Foster** in her triumphant turn as *Thoroughly Modern Millie*. Since then the triple threat has charmed Broadway audiences by playing a writer, a princess, a movie star, a nightclub singer, and a Transylvania farm girl. Now the two-time Tony winner is conquering television in the acclaimed series *Bunheads*. A children's biography, ***Sutton Foster: Broadway Sweetheart, TV Bunhead*** details the role model's rise from a tiny ballerina to the toast of Broadway and Hollywood.

Idina Menzel's career has been "Defying Gravity" for years! With starring roles in *Wicked* and *Rent*, the Tony-winner is one of theater's most beloved performers. The powerful vocalist has also branched out in other mediums. She has filmed a recurring role on television's smash hit *Glee* and lent her talents to the Disney films, *Enchanted* and *Frozen*. A children's biography, ***Idina Menzel: Broadway Superstar*** narrates the actress' rise to fame from a Long Island wedding singer to overnight success!

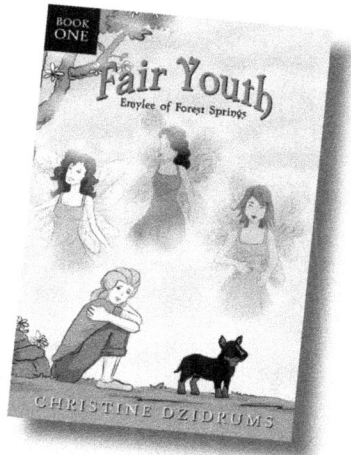

Twelve-year-old Emylee Markette has felt invisible her entire life. Then one fateful afternoon, three beautiful sisters arrive in her sleepy New England town and instantly become the most popular girls at Forest Springs Middle School. To everyone's surprise, the Fay sisters befriend Emylee and welcome her into their close-knit circle. Before long, the shy loner finds herself running with the cool crowd, joining the track team and even becoming friends with her lifelong crush.

Through it all, though, Emylee's weighed down by nagging suspicions. Why were the Fay sisters so anxious to befriend her? How do they know some of her inner thoughts? What do they truly want from her?

When Emylee eventually discovers that her new friends are secretly fairies, she finds her life turned upside down yet again and must make some life-changing decisions.

Fair Youth: Emylee of Forest Springs marks the first volume in an exciting new book series.

Ashley Moore wants to know why there's never been a girl president. Before long the inspired six-year-old creates a special, girls-only club - the **Future Presidents Club**. Meet five enthusiastic young girls who are ready to change the world. *Future Presidents Club: Girls Rule* is the first book in a series about girls making a difference!

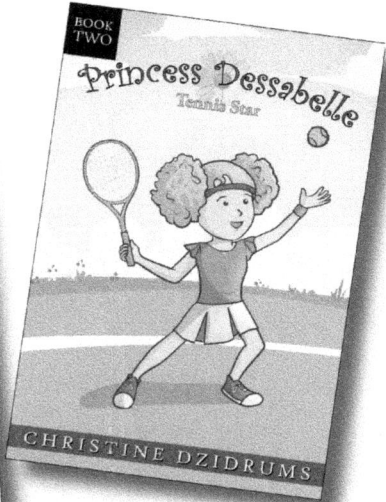

Meet **Princess Dessabelle**, a spoiled, lonely princess with a quick temper.

In *Princess Dessabelle Makes a Friend,* the lonely youngster discovers the meaning of true friendship. *Princess Dessabelle: Tennis Star* finds the pampered girl learning the importance of good sportsmanship.

Quinn
The Ballerina
The Sleeping Beau y

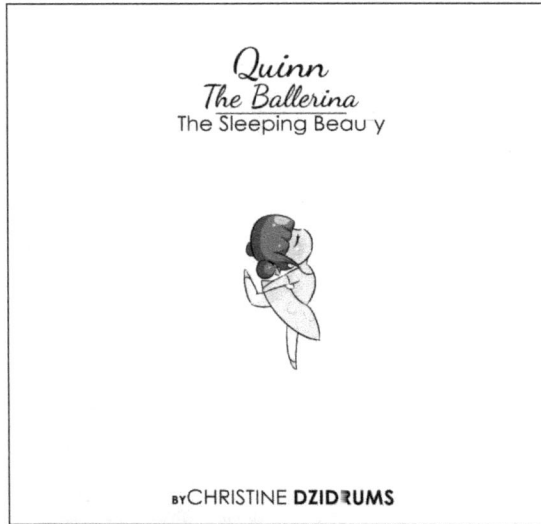

BY CHRISTINE **DZIDRUMS**

Quinn the Ballerina can hardly believe it's finally performance day. She's playing her first principal role in a production of *The Sleeping Beauty*.

Yet, Quinn is also nervous. Can she really dance the challenging steps? Will people believe her as a cursed princess caught in a 100-year spell?

Join Quinn as she transforms into Princess Aurora in an exciting retelling of Tchaikovsky's *The Sleeping Beauty*. Now you can relive, or experience for the first time, one of ballet's most acclaimed works as interpreted by a 9 year old.

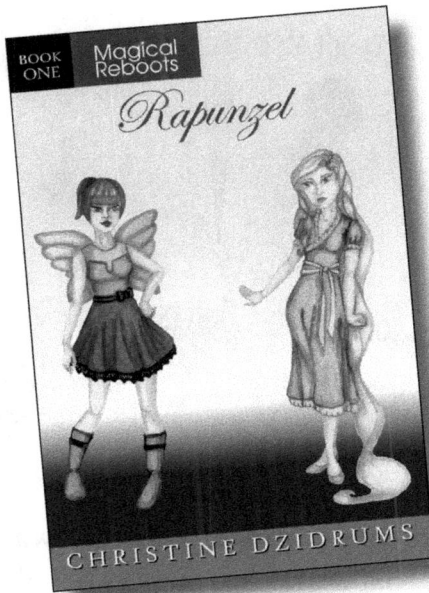

From the popular new series, ***Classical Reboots,*** ***Rapunzel*** updates the **Brothers Grimm** fairy tale with hilarious and heartbreaking results.

Rapunzel has been locked in her adoptive mother's attic for years. Just as the despondent teenager abandons hope of escaping her private prison, a mysterious tablet computer appears. Before long, Rapunzel's quirky fairy godmother, Aiko, has the conflicted young girl questioning her place in the world.

Cutters Don't Cry

2010 Moonbeam Children's Book Award Winner! In a series of raw journal entries written to her absentee father, a teenager chronicles her penchant for self-harm, a serious struggle with depression and an inability to vocally express her feelings.

Kaylee: The 'What If?' Game

"I play the 'What If?'" game all the time. It's a cruel, wicked game."

When free spirit Kaylee suffers a devastating loss, her personality turns dark as she struggles with depression and unresolved anger. Can Kaylee repair her broken spirit, or will she remain a changed person?